A Legal Binding Agreement™

[APPROVED BY A TWO-PARTY DECISION]

-An original document Created by-

Courtney Lazalier

DEDICATION

IF EVER IN A SITUATION THAT THE TWO PARTY
CANNOT COME TO AN AGREEMENT;
THIS DOCUMENT WAS CREATED TO RESOLVE ANY
CONFLICTS BETWEEN A TWO PARTY DISPUTE. THE
TWO PARTIES LISTED IN THIS DOCUMENT NO
LONGER SHARE A RELATIONSHIP THAT CONNECTS
THEIR PARENTAL DECISION MAKING RIGHTS AS ONE
EQUAL DECISION.

GRANTED, THEY STILL ACKNOWLEDGE THE
REPONSIBILITY AND IMPORTANCE OF DEVELOPING A
SEPARATED AND EQUAL AGREEMENT.

THIS DOCUMENT GIVES EXAMPLE TO AND ALSO
STANDS AS A POSSIBLE FUTURE REFERENCE. AS IT IS A
GUIDELINE WITH RULES AND REGULATIONS THAT
THE TWO MUST LIVE BY IF EVER IN A SITUATION
THAT RESULTS WITH FILING A DISPUTE CASE WITHIN
THE COURTS SYSTEM.

THIS DOCUMENT ONLY STANDS AS EVIDENCE
TO BOTH PARTIES AGREEING TO BOTH SHARE A JOINT
CUSTODY BETWEEN THE TWO PARTY. THE TWO
PARTIES IN THIS DOCUMENT ARE THE RIGHTFUL
PARENTS OF THE MINOR CHILD AND HAS BEEN
ESTABLISHED PATERNITY OVER THE CHILD BY
SIGNING AN AFFIDAVIT WHICH ESTABLISHES
PARTERNITY OF THE CHILD.

Table of Contents

♥♣Bonus Features♣♥

Things To Do List
Contact List
To Show Appreciation Certificate
2016-2017 Yearly Calendar
Previous Yearly Calendars, Since Carson's Birth
Notes
Contact Information To The Author
The Very Selfish Giant

THE PURPOSE OF THIS DOCUMENT AND ITS LEGAL VALUE

DO NOT FILE THIS AGREEMENT WITH THE COURTS SYSTEM. THE ONLY REASON TO IGNORE THIS IS IF BOTH PARTIES CANNOT COME TO AN AGREEMENT. THEN AS TO SOLVE THE TWO PARTIES DISAGREEMENT, THIS OFFICIAL DOCUMENT SHOULD THEN ACT AS A THE RESOURCE TO GUIDELINES AND PROCEDURES TO FOLLOW IN THE COURT OF LAW FOR THE JUDGE TO MAKE HIS DECISION.

As The Rightful Introduction to This Document;
I provide to you the Equal and Mutual Understanding of What Rights You Are Given Along With This Legal Binding Agreement. Please Acknowledge That This Document Will Not Be Represented In Front Of A Judge In The Court Of The Law. Therefore You Are Given The Authority To Having The Right To Hire An Attorney, As There Will Not Be One Appointed To You. Notice That After You Sign This Document, It Is Then A Legal Binding Agreement As Well As A Contract. Having The Right To Hire An Attorney For Their Professional Advice Before Signing This Document Is The Rightful Given Decision That Would Be Solemnly Made By You. As Your Signature Represents Your Agreement To Everything On This Legal Binding Agreement.

This Is A Legal Binding Agreement Between A Two Party Decisions For A Joint-Custody Agreement. Only After Each Party Has Read This Document And If They Agree To Everything Stated Within This Document, Then Must Represent This Understanding By Signing This Agreement. Which Implies That You Have The Knowledge To All Of Its Contents For Which If You Signed This Agreement In Front Of A Public Notary Having And Waived Any And All Disputes Or Rights Within Its Guidelines To Not Having. You May Hire An Attorney To Give His Legal Advice Before Signing This Agreement. However, A Lawyer Will Not Be Appointed To You As Representation To The Court Of Law As This Agreement Will Not Be Presented In The Presence Of A Judge. Exceptions May Exist, As This Agreement May Later Be Used As A Reference For Future References. Therefore, You Have No Rights To An Attorney, But May Address One Yourself If You Wish Before Giving Your Signature.

IF BOTH PARTIES HAVE SIGNED THIS DOCUMENT, THEY ADMIT TO EVERYTHING WITHIN THIS DOCUMENT TO BE TRUE.

This Legal Binding Agreement Was Published To Give The Ease Of Access To Whomever May Need The Information To The Listed Child Of This Documents Custody Case. As Well As To Not Having The Option To Alter Any Guidelines Within Its Contents. The Only Exception To This Rule Is If Both Parties Agree To Make A Change In Its Contents. Acceptable Only if Both Parties Sign The Last Page In This Binding Agreement. The Signature Must Be Signed As To Make A Notion, Witnessed By A Public Notary And Another Volume Will Be Added To This Original Document. The Next Volume Will Contain The Extended Data They Both Agree Upon With Signature To Another Volume Of Its Series. Numerous Copies Can Be Obtained But Is Only Valid If It Contains Each Parties Signature In Witness Of A Public Notary.

The Courts Rights

The court does NOT have jurisdiction over the custody arrangements of the minor child pursuant to the Uniform Child Custody Jurisdiction and Enforcement Act. Along with the Legal Binding Agreement the two party have knowledge to signing as to not bringing extra enforcement into the child's custody case. Therefore enters no further orders with respect to the custodial agreement and arrangements of the Minor child. This agreement is only proposed and signed by each party for future references to act as guideline and procedures to follow if either party cannot come to an agreement at which then they decide to further their rights to a circuit court and by law represented in the court of the law in front of a judge to end all dispute and bring them to an equal agreement.

INTRODUCING EACH PARTY AND WHAT RIGHTS THEY HAVE

The Two Party Decision of a Legal Binding Agreement

One out of the two parties receiving joint custody
Courtney Nicole Lazalier – Mother of the child.
One out of the two parties receiving joint custody
Ethan Michael Tinsley- Father of the child

The Child Of Which Binds The Two Party Together

The one and only child they share

Carson Matthew Tinsley – First son

The 6 Mediators &Their Relationship To The Child

One out of the six mediators – grandmother
Rushell Kay Lazalier

One out of the six mediators - grandfather
Scott Edward Lazalier

One out of the six mediators - grandmother
Carla Jean Williamson

One out of the six mediators - grandfather
Jeff Williamson

One out of the six mediators - grandfather
Russell Tinsley

One out of the six mediators – great grandmother
Joan Johnson

To Act As Caretaker In The Last Living Will

Carla Williamson & Rushell Lazalier

Power of Attorney

Courtney Lazalier

213 Seventh St.

Farmington Mo. 63640

573-561-3849

Dated_____

To Whom It May Concern:

I am the parent of Carson Matthew Tinsley and I do hereby give my permission to and appoint

_____as temporary guardian(s) of my minor child only to make any and all necessary decisions about my child's health care. Said temporary guardians shall have Sincereness , of the rights to choosing and authorizing medical treatment for my child at this time period as I have as a parent.

Courtney Lazalier

(Please only except this note if it is actually signed and dated by the mother of Carson Tinsley.)

Power of Attorney

Ethan Tinsley
1283 Madison 209.
Fredericktown Mo. 63645

Dated_____

To Whom It May Concern:

I am the parent of Carson Matthew Tinsley and I do hereby give my permission to and appoint _____ As temporary guardian(s) of my minor child only to make any and all necessary decisions about my child's health care. Said temporary guardians shall have all of the rights to choosing and authorizing medical treatment for my child at this time period as I have as a parent.

Sincerely,

Ethan Tinsley

(Please only except this note if it is actually signed and dated by the father of Carson Tinsley.)

THE LEGAL BINDING AGREEMENT.™

DECISION FOR A JOINT-CUSTODY

The Parents Information

MOTHERS FULL NAME IS:

COURTNEY

NICOLE

LAZALIER

THIS IS THE ORIGINAL DOCUMENT,

CREATED BY:

COURTNEY

NICOLE

LAZALIER

HER MAILING ADRESS IS:

_____

_____

_____

TELEPHONE NUMBER:

_____

FATHERS FULL NAME IS:

Ethan

Michael

Tinsley

HIS MAILING ADDRESS:

_____

_____

_____

TELEPHONE NUMBER:

_____

Service Information

Both parties have signed a verified "Answer to Decision for Determination of Custody" which brings this document to a legal binding motion. Therefore, do not issue a Summons or address this document to the courts system unless there is a decision neither parties can come to an agreement on. It's also recommended to do what is needed of each party to qualify for benefits received; all rules by any division of Social Services apply.

They currently are not receiving Temporary Assistance for Needy Families (TANF);
They are currently receiving Food Stamps;
They are currently receiving Medicaid

Case Information

I AM ENTITLED TO ESTABLISH OUR CLAIM IN SPLITTING OUR RIGHTS FOR A JOINT-CUSTODY AGREEMENT BECAUSE: PATERNITY WAS ACKNOWLEDGED BY BOTH PARTIES AND FATHER'S NAME APPEARS ON THE BIRTH CERTIFICATE OF EACH CHILD LISTED IN THIS PETITION.

The Child Pertaining to This Agreements Information

NAME:

CARSON

MATTHEW

TINSLEY

PARENTS OF THIS CHILD ESTABLISHED BY SIGNATURE ON THE CHILD'S AFFIDAVIT LEGALLY ESTABLISHING PATERNITY

MOTHER AS,

COURTNEY

NICOLE

LAZALIER

FATHER AS,

ETHAN

MICHAEL

TINSLEY

DATE & PLACE OF BIRTH

_____

—

==============================.

@ _____HOSPITAL

IN _____ COUNTY

FARMINGTON, MO.

THE CHILD'S MAILING ADDRESS

IT HAS BEEN DECIDED AND BOTH PARTIES AGREE TO AS BEING IN THE CHILD'S BEST INTEREST THAT THE CHILD'S MAILING ADDRESS BE THE SAME MAILING ADDRESS AS THE MOTHERS MAILING ADDRESS. AS THE MOTHER HAS CLAIMED THE CHILD LIVING THERE THROUGH THE SOCIAL SERVICES SUPPORTS DIVISION. AS THEY ARE CURRENTLY RECEIVING MEDICAID AND FOOD STAMPS THROUGH SOCIAL SERVICES AS LIVING UNDER THE SAME RESIDENCY AS THE MOTHER.

BOTH PARTIES SIGNITURE TO AN AGREEMENT

SIGNATURE BY BOTH PARTIES, AS WELL AS A SIGNATURE BY A PUBLIC

NOTARY TO REPRESENT AS A WITNESS TO THE TWO PARTY SIGNING THIS

DOCUMENT PUTS THIS LEGAL BINDING AGREEMENT INTO MOTION.

AS THE MOTHER OF CARSON MATTHEW TINSLEY, I HEREBY ESTABLISH TO
HAVE REACHED A COMPLETE AND AUTHORIZED DECISION UPON THE
GUARDIAN CUSTODIAN FOR MY CHILD. AWARE BY GIVING THE AGREED
UPON DECISION OF A JOINT-CUSTODY AGREEMENT BETWEEN THE
ESTABLISHED FATHER, WHO IS RIGHTFULLY BY LAW REPRESENTED BY HIS
SIGNATURE ON THE AFFIDAVIT ESTABLISHING PATERNITY AS THE
FATHER ON THE CHILD'S BIRTH CERTIFICATE AND MYSELF. SIGNING THIS
DOCUMENT IN FRONT OF THIS NOTARY TODAY, GIVES MY KNOWLEDGE AND
LAW GIVING RIGHT TO HAVING EACH OF US BOTH EQUAL RIGHTS, EQUAL
DECISION MAKING RIGHTS, EQUAL AUTHORITY OVER, AND ENTITLEMENT BY
LAW TO HAVING AS WELL AS GIVING ANY AND ALL INFORMATION TO MY
KNOWLEDGE THAT PERTAINS TO

THE ABOVE LISTED CHILD TO AND FROM THE OTHER PARTY AS WELL.
MAKING THIS A LEGAL BINDING AGREEMENT AS WE DO NOT NEED
INVOLVEMENT OF THE COURTS SYSTEM IN OUR RELATIONS PERTAINING TO
OUR CHILD. HOWEVER, IF THIS DOCUMENTS REQUIRES ADDITIONAL
AUTHORITY MATTERS FOR FUTURE REFERENCES WE MAY INCLUDE THE
COURT'S DECISION BASED UPON THE DOCUMENTS ORIGINAL DOCUMENTED
AGREEMENT OF WHICH THE TWO PARTIES HAVE SIGNED TO.

X_____

(One out of the Two Party Agreement as A Legal Custodian's Signature)

AS THE FATHER OF CARSON MATTHEW TINSLEY, WHO IS RIGHTFULLY BY LAW REPRESENTED BY HIS SIGNATURE ON THE AFFIDAVIT ESTABLISHING PATERNITY AS THE FATHER ON THE CHILD'S BIRTH CERTIFICATE HAS ESTABLISHED TO HAVE REACHED A COMPLETE AND AUTHORIZED DECISION UPON THE GUARDIAN CUSTODIAN FOR MY CHILD. AWARE BY GIVING THE AGREED UPON DECISION OF A JOINT-CUSTODY AGREEMENT BETWEEN THE ESTABLISHED MOTHER, WHO IS RIGHTFULLY BY LAW REPRESENTED BY HER SIGNATURE ON THE AFFIDAVIT ESTABLISHING PATERNITY AS THE MOTHER ON THE CHILD'S BIRTH CERTIFICATE AND MYSELF. SIGNING THIS DOCUMENT IN FRONT OF THIS NOTARY TODAY, GIVES MY KNOWLEDGE AND LAW GIVING RIGHT TO HAVING EACH OF US BOTH EQUAL RIGHTS, EQUAL DECISION MAKING RIGHTS, EQUAL AUTHORITY OVER, AND ENTITLEMENT BY LAW TO HAVING AS WELL AS GIVING ANY AND ALL INFORMATION TO MY KNOWLEDGE THAT PERTAINS TO THE ABOVE LISTED CHILD TO AND FROM THE OTHER PARTY AS WELL. MAKING THIS A LEGAL BINDING AGREEMENT AS WE DO NOT NEED INVOLVEMENT OF THE COURTS SYSTEM IN OUR RELATIONS PERTAINING TO OUR CHILD. HOWEVER, IF THIS DOCUMENTS REQUIRES ADDITIONAL AUTHORITY MATTERS FOR FUTURE REFERENCES WE MAY INCLUDE THE COURT'S DECISION BASED UPON THE DOCUMENTS ORIGINAL DOCUMENTED AGREEMENT OF WHICH THE TWO PARTIES HAVE SIGNED TO

.X_____ *(One out of the*

Two Party Agreement as A Legal Custodian's Signature)

I, A Public Notary have witnessed before me, both parties signatures Signed in front of me; on this day of _____ on _____, the year of 20_____ in the county of _____ and state of

_____.

X_____

(Signature of Public Notary)

THE PARENTING PLAN

Duration of this agreement

The terms and conditions set forth in this parenting plan shall remain in full force and effect until the child is emancipated or until this plan is modified by both party's knowledge and agreement. If the two party can't come to an agreement then the terms and/or conditions set forth in this plan by be altered by a court of competent jurisdiction.

Decisions Concerning the Child

"Joint legal custody" means that the parents share the decision making rights, responsibilities, and authority relating to the health, education and welfare of the child, and, unless allocated, apportioned, or decreed, the Parents shall <u>confer</u> with one another in the exercise of decision-making rights, responsibilities, and authority.

Types of Decisions

MAJOR DECISIONS,

- ➢ THE CHOICE OR CHANGE OF SCHOOLS, INCLUDING COLLEGE OR SPECIAL TUTORING
- ➢ THE CHOICE OR CHANGE OF PHYSICIAN, SURGEON, OR DENTIST
- ➢ RELIGIOUS INSTRUCTION, TRAINING OR EDUCATION
- ➢ SELECTION OF CHILD CARE PROVIDERS
- ➢ SELECTION OF CHILD, SURGERY, OR ANY MEDICAL CARE, SURGERY, OR ANY MEDICAL PROCEDURE REQUIRING HOSPITALIZATION OR OUT-PATIENT SURGERY.
- ➢ MAJOR DENTAL WORK AND ORTHODONTIST
- ➢ PSYCHOLOGICAL OR PSYCHIATRIC TREATMENT OR COUNSELING

> ➢ THE CHOICE OR CHANGE OF CAMPS OR OTHER SPECIAL OR EXTRACURRICULAR ACTIVITIES
> ➢ The extent of any travel away from home,
> ➢ Part or full-time employment,
>
> ➢ Purchase or operation of a motor vehicle,
> ➢ Contraception and sex education,
> ➢ Actual or potential litigation on behalf of the children.

DAILY OR EVERYDAY DECISIONS,

Daily or everyday decisions are routine decisions, like minor medical treatment, bedtimes, homework, Chores, selection of clothing and normal daily activities. Daily decisions shall be made by the parent having actual physical custody at the time of the decision. The Parents shall cooperate in establishing mutually agreeable policies regarding such decisions in order that routine decisions remain as consistent as possible.

EMERGENCY DECISIONS

Emergency decisions are decisions of an urgent nature. They affect the health and safety of the child and have to be made before it is possible to contact the other parent. The parent who is with the minor child requiring emergency care may make the emergency decision. The Parent making the emergency decision shall advise the other parent of the nature and extent of the emergency as Soon as possible.

ACCESS TO MEDICAL, DENTAL, & EDUCATIONAL RECORDS OF THE CHILD

BOTH PARENTS ARE ENTITLED TO ACCESS TO RECORDS AND INFORMATION THAT PERTAINS TO THE CHILD, INCLUDING, BUT NOT LIMITED TO, FULL AND COMPLETE MEDICAL, DENTAL, AND EDUCATIONAL RECORDS.

LEGAL CUSTODY

AS A LEGAL BINDING AGREEMENT, BOTH PARTIES AGREE TO A JOINT LEGAL CUSTODY, THAT DOESN'T NEED ANY HIGHER AUTHORITY LEVELS OR A COURTS SYSTEM INVOLVED WITH THIS DECISION. AS BOTH PARTIES ARE AWARE AND AGREE TO THIS LEGAL CUSTODY DECISION AND IT IS IN THE BEST INTERESTS OF THE CHILDREN THAT MOTHER AND FATHER HAVE JOINT LEGAL CUSTODY OF THE CHILD. MAJOR DECISIONS SHALL BE MADE BY MOTHER AND FATHER JOINTLY. IF MOTHER AND FATHER DISAGREE ON A MAJOR DECISION THEY SHALL RESOLVE THEIR DISAGREEMENT THROUGH THE DISPUTE RESOLUTION PROCEDURE SET FORTH HEREIN. FOLLOWED THEN BY HIGH AUTHORITY LEVELS IF STILL IN DISPUTE.

Issues not to be discussed in the Presence of the Child

Mother and Father shall each refrain from making negative, derogatory or degrading statements about the other parent in front of the child. Both parents shall exercise their best efforts to foster the respect, love and affection of the children toward the other parent. Mother and Father shall avoid discussing parenting issues, financial issues, and other topics related to these proceedings when the children are present. Mother and Father should prevent other persons from making negative, derogatory or degrading statements about the other parent in the presence of the child.

When the Children Will Be with Each Parent

"Joint physical custody"

An order awarding each of the parents significant but not necessarily equal, periods of time during which a child resides with or is under the care and supervision of each of the parents. Joint physical custody shall be shared by the parents in such a way as to assure the child of frequent, continuing and meaningful contact with both parents

JOINT PHYSICAL CUSTODY USING THE MOTHER'S ADDRESS

Residential Schedules

MOTHER AND FATHER SHALL BOTH SHARE PHYSICAL CUSTODY

MOTHER AND FATHER SHALL EXCHANGE THE CHILD AS SET FORTH IN THE RESIDENTIAL SCHEDULES. EACH PARENT SHALL CONSIDER REASONABLE CHANGES WHEN REQUESTED BY THE OTHER PARENT OR THE CHILD SIGNIFICANT CHANGE IS MADE, EITHER PARENT MAY REDUCE THEIR AGREEMENT TO WRITING. ALL CHANGES ARE UNENFORCEABLE unless in writing and signed by both parents

Transportation

THE PARENT RECEIVING THE CHILD IS RESPONSIBLE FOR TRANSPORTING THE   CHILD TO THE EXCHANGE LOCATION.

EACH PARTY WILL PAY THE EXPENSES ASSOCIATED WITH HIS OR HER OWN TRANSPORTATION TO AND FROM THE EXCHANGE LOCATION UNLESS OTHERWISE INDICATED IN THIS PARENTING PLAN.

Notification of change from residential schedule

IN THE EVENT EITHER PARENT CANNOT EXERCISE THE SCHEDULED TIME WITH THE CHILD HE OR SHE SHOULD TELL THE OTHER PARENT AS SOON AS POSSIBLE, BUT NOT LATER THAN 24 HOURS BEFORE THE START OF THE SCHEDULED TIME WITH THE CHILD. IF A PARENT ANTICIPATES THAT HE OR SHE

MAY HAVE TO CANCEL AT THE LAST MINUTE, HE OR SHE SHOULD ADVISE THE OTHER PARENT OF THE POSSIBLE LAST MINUTE CONFLICT. IF A PARENT FAILS TO NOTIFY THE OTHER PARTY AS SET FORTH ABOVE, HE OR SHE SHALL BE RESPONSIBLE FOR THE REASONABLE COSTS INCURRED BY THE OTHER PARENT.

Child's Activities

BOTH PARENTS MUST ATTEMPT TO ACCOMMODATE THE SOCIAL AND ACADEMIC COMMITMENTS OF THE CHILD. EACH PARENT SHOULD ATTEMPT TO REFRAIN FROM SCHEDULING ACTIVITIES THAT OCCUR PRIMARILY WHEN THE CHILDREN ARE WITH THE OTHER PARENT. IF AN ACTIVITY WILL AFFECT THE OTHER PARENT'S TIME WITH THE CHILD, THE PARENT SCHEDULING THE ACTIVITY SHOULD OBTAIN THE AFFECTED PARENT'S PERMISSION BEFORE COMMITTING THE CHILD TO THE ACTIVITY.

Dispute Resolution Procedure

This is the manner in which Mother and Father will Resolve Disagreements Concerning The Child.

This Includes disagreements on the meaning or interpretation of any provision of this plan. Mother and Father shall present their disagreements to a mediator as a temporary decision until a binding mediation hearing is held within the families own arranged location. The hearing process is to give both parties the right to voice and argue their side to the disagreement. Then giving them the right to vote to an agreement as to the child's resolution. . In the event that the parents cannot resolve the dispute by mediation that is when they must settle the family feud through the Courts system. As this is a Legal binding agreement to this child's custody case, that means the judge must come to a decision based along the guidelines this agreement contains, as the two party have the knowledge to signing and have already agreed to these rules and regulations.

RELOCATION

EACH PARTY BY SIGNING THIS LEGAL BINDING AGREEMENT GIVE THE KNOWLEDGE TO KNOWING THEY ARE TO NOTIFY, IN WRING BY MAIL OR AT A MEETING OF THE PROPOSED RELOCATION BEFORE ACTUALLY MOVING TO THE PROPOSED RELOCATION AREA. THE LETTER MUST CONTAIN THE FOLLOWING INFORMATION:

- ➢ THE INTENDED NEW RESIDENCE, INCLUDING THE SPECIFIC ADDRESS AND MAILING ADDRESS, IF KNOWN, AND IF NOT KNOWN THE CITY.
- ➢ THE HOME TELEPHONE NUMBER OF THE NEW RESIDENCE IS APPLICABLE
- ➢ THE DATE OF THE INTENDED MOVE TO THE RELOCATION AREA
- ➢ IF THE PARTY WISHES TO ADD THE REASON THEY MAY, HOWEVER IF IT INVOLVES A THREAT OR NEED TO KNOW FOR THE SAFETY OF THE CHILD THEY MUST GIVE FORTH THAT

INFORMATION, OTHERWISE THAT PARTY COULD LATER

RESULT IN A CHILD ENDANGERMENT. BASED UPON NOT GIVING THE OTHER PARTY RIGHTFUL INFORMATION LIMITING THE OTHER PARTY THE ABILITY TO EFFECT THE SAFETY PROCEDURE OF THE CHILD TO CREATE A SAFE LIVING

ENVIRONMENT. AS LONG AS THE PARTY AT THE LEAST INFORMS THE NON-SAFETY REASON THEY WILL NOT AFFECT

NEGATIVELY BY IT. MEANING THEY STILL HAVE THE PARENTAL RIGHT TO THE CHILD AND ARE LEGALLY ABLE TO DO WITH THE CHILD AS THEY PLEASE ON THEIR DAYS OF

HAVING THAT CHILD. STILL THE OTHER PARTY HAS THE LEGAL RIGHT OF KNOWING THE SITUATION OF THE CHILD AS WELL.

➤ PROPOSAL FOR A REVISED SCHEDULE OF CUSTODY OR VISITATION WITH THE CHILD.

YOU'RE OBLIGATION

TO PROVIDE THIS INFORMATION TO EACH PARTY CONTINUES

AS LONG AS YOU OR ANY OTHER PARTY BY VIRTUE OF THIS

AGREEMENT IS ENTITLED TO CUSTODY OF A CHILD COVERED

BY THIS ORDER. YOUR FAILURE TO OBEY THIS AGREEMENT

MAY RESULT IN FURTHER LITIGATION TO ENFORCE SUCH

ORDER BY PETITIONING THE CHILD'S CUSTODY IN THE COURT

OF LAW IN FRONT OF A JUDGE.

Mon	Tues	Wed	Thurs	Fri	Sat	Sun
M STARTS AT 2:00	*M*	*F*	*F*	*W* STARTS AT 2:00	*W*	*W*

W -represents a weekend day

F – Fathers residential stay

M – Mothers residential stay

Residential schedules (continued)

WEEKEND AND WEEKDAY SCHEDULE

AS THE HEAD START SCHOOL SCHEDULE THE TWO PARTY HAS AGREED TO EQUALLY SPLITTING THE PHYSICAL CUSTODY OF THE CHILD. HAVING THE WEEK DAYS SPLIT EQUALLY, AS WELL AS SPLITTING EVERY OTHER WEEKEND. EACH PARTY HAS THE RIGHT TO HAVING THE CHILD, UNLESS FOR WHATEVER REASON THEY CANNOT TAKE THE CHILD. REGARDING TO THIS MAY ALSO HAVE ALTERNATIVE PROPOSALS TO SWITCHING ONE WEEKEND FOR ANOTHER OR ANY OTHER ALTERCATIONS TO THE SCHEDULE, WHICH MAY BE ACCEPTABLE AS LONG AS THE OTHER PARTY AGREES TO THE PROPOSAL.

THE WEEKEND

INVOLVES WHEN THE CHILD GETS OUT OF SCHOOL AT 2:00 P.M. ON FRIDAY, SATURDAY, AND SUNDAY. THESE ARE THE DAYS THAT WILL BE ALTERNATED BETWEEN THE TWO PARTIES. TIME WITH THE GRANDPARENTS, IF AT ANOTHER LOCATION OTHER THAN THE PARENT WITH VISITATION TIME, MUST NOTICE THAT THEY WILL HAVE TO NEGOTIATE TIME WITHIN THEIR OWN CHILD'S SCHEDULE WITH THE CHILD. WHICHEVER HAS PARENTAL AUTHORITY OVER THE CHILD THAT WEEKEND IS DESIGNATED BETWEEN THAT PARENT AND THAT SET OF GRANDPARENTS AND VICE VERSA. NO COUNTER PARENT AND GRANDPARENT SHOULD HAVE A DISPUTE BETWEEN THE SCHEDULING.

DURING THE WEEK,

IT IS INSISTED THAT THE CHILD, UNLESS THEY PARTY CANNOT TRANSFER OR HAS SOME REASON FOR NOT BE ABLE TO CARE FOR THE CHILD IS MOTHERS MONDAY AT 2:00. THIS IS TO KEEP SAME TIME SWITCH AND CHANGES EQUAL. WHICH IS THE SAME AS ANY OTHER SCHOOL DAY. THIS WILL ALSO BENEFIT THE CHILD TO INSURE HE IS READY FOR SCHOOL THAT WEEK.

VACATION SCHEDULE

EACH PARTY IS LEGALLY GIVEN THE RIGHT TO HAVING THE CHILD, UNLESS NEGOTIATED OTHERWISE, EVERY OTHER MAJOR HOLIDAY, MINOR HOLIDAYS AREN'T NECESSARY TO CHANGE THE SCHEDULE OF THE CHILD'S NORMAL PARENTAL WEEK SCHEDULE.

EXCEPT FOR CHRISTMAS, THIS HOLIDAY IS TO BE A SPLIT HOLIDAY, -

ROTATING BETWEEN THE TWO PARTY EQUALLY EACH YEAR GRANTING THEM THE BENEFIT OF WAKING UP CHRISTMAS DAY AT THEIR HOUSE. HOWEVER, THE TWO PARTY SHOULD NEGOTIATE THE DAY BEFORE CHRISTMAS AS AN OFFERING TO SPEND THE HOLIDAY SEASON WITH THE OPPOSING PARTY AS WELL.

MOTHER'S DAY AND FATHER'S DAY; SHOULD BE OFFERED AS BENEFIT EACH PARENTS SCHEDULE FOR THEIR DAY.

DURING THE SUMMER;

WHENEVER THERE IS NO LONGER ANY SCHOOL DAYS THAT THE CHILD MUST ATTEND THEN THE CHILD WILL RESIDE WITH ONE PARTY FOR ONE WEEK AND THEN THE OTHER PARTY FOR ONE WEEK. THIS IS TO TAKE EFFECT UNTIL THE CHILD IS OLD ENOUGH AND AGREED BY BOTH PARTIES AS ABLE TO COME TO A DECISION BASED UPON HIS CHOICE OF ANOTHER PLAN. WHICH WILL BE WRITTEN IN AN ALTERED AGREEMENT AS ANOTHER VOLUME TO THIS SERIES AND SIGNED BY BOTH PARTIES IN THIS AGREEMENT. HOWEVER, THIS CANNOT TAKE EFFECT IF THE CHILD IS ONLY HAVING ALTERCATIONS MADE OUT OF ANGER TOWARDS THE OTHER PARTY.

<u>EXAMPLES TO HAVING REASONABLE ALTERCATIONS WOULD BE</u>:

A CAMP HE IS WANTING TO ATTEND, A SPORT THAT HAS PRACTICE DURING CERTAIN TIMING OF THE SUMMER, A FRIEND IN A LIVING ENVIRONMENT THAT HAS A SCHEDULE ENFORCED VISITATION AS WELL AND STILL WOULD LIKE TO PLAY WITH, ETC. HOWEVER THE REVISED SCHEDULE HAS TO PERTAIN TO EQUAL VISITATION BETWEEN THE TWO PARTY FOR THAT SUMMER.

<u>BEST INTEREST</u>;

IT'S BETTER TO BE NON-GREEDY AND TO BE THOUGHTFUL AS TO SOMEHOW ALL WORKING TOGETHER IN ORDER TO ALL HAVE TIME, MEMORIES, AND WELL-KEPT FAMILY TIMES. AS A ROUTINE MIND SET, TRY TO THINK OF WAYS BOTH FAMILIES MAY PARTICIPATE HAVING THE CHILD IN THEIR PRESENCE FOR ANY OCCASION.

NOTE: If the child can not handle the schedule and starts failing classes , then he must attend more at one designated place. Either with the mother or the father, this excludes living arrangements designated to a grandparents home stay unless the mother or father resides with a grandparent. whichever is in the best interest of the child. Routine schedules will then start as during week days residing at one parents and then every weekend with the other parent. Except for one weekend during the month will be spent with the designated weekday parent. To better his education for school

INCOME AND EXPENSE STATMENT

Child support and expenses

No regular monthly child support will be paid by either parent. Father will be referred to as "person paying support" and Mother will be referred to as "person receiving support." For the purpose of the Form 14 Child support calculation only.

Medical and Dental Insurance for the child

AS THE MOTHER IS THE GUARDIAN WHO WENT TO THE SOCIAL SERVICES OFFICE TO APPLY FOR THE CHILD'S INSURANCE THEY MUST FOLLOW THE PROCEDURE MADE BY THE SOCIAL SERVICES DIRECTORY TO KEEP THE CHILD'S MEDICARE. THE FOLLOWING INFORMATION IS WHAT HAS BEEN PROVIDED FOR THE CHILD.

THE CHILD'S MEDICAL INFORMATION:

NAME: _____

MO HEALTH NET ID _____

PCP NAME _____

PCP ADDRESS: _____

PCP PHONE # _____

- IF THE INSURANCE LATER HAS BEEN CHANGED OR ANOTHER METHOD IS TAKEN TO CONSIDERATION THEN THE AGREEMENT MUST BE ALTERED AND NOTED AND SIGNED AGAIN AS TO SPLIT THE COST WITH THE OTHER PARTY.

- Neither party is required to maintain medical insurance for the child. A health benefit Plan is not available at reasonable cost through either parent's employer or union. Support rights have been assigned to the state of Missouri and the Family Support Division is providing support enforcement services to the mother.

Health expenses not covered by insurance

Pertaining to: MEDICAL, DENTAL, VISION, OR

PSYCHOLOGICAL EXPENSES NOT COVERED BY INSURANCE;

AFTER THE INSURANCE HAS PAID FOR THE COST, THE REMAINDER PORTION OF THE BILL WILL THEN BE LEFT TO WHICHEVER GUARDIAN HAS THE CHILD, UNLESS IT IS A LARGE SUM OF MONEY THAT NEITHER PARTY COULD HELP FROM BEING BILLED, THEN THE TWO PARTY MUST SPLIT THE BILL. POSSIBLE REASONS NOT TO SPLIT THE BILL WOULD BE AN ACCIDENT WITH AN E.R. BILL FOR OWN FAULT REASONS.

E.R. BILLS THAT ARE BECAUSE OF THE CHILD BEING SICK WILL NEED TO BE ADDED AT EACH PARTY AND COMPARED TO THE OTHER PARTY COMPLETE SUM AND WHATEVER THE DIFFERENCE IS THE TWO PARTY WILL MAY SPLIT THE DIFFERENCE OR TRADE EXPENSES WITH.

School Support And Costs

Each party will provide for the child as needed equally. If one party decides the cost isn't fair, they will be asked to save all receipts to come up with the total sum of all school support costs as to compare costs with the other party. To overall resolve the dispute they will then split the cost equally. However, no consequences are given if ever one party isn't able to pay an equal matching price. They either will have to come to a mutual agreement of eliminating what the cost over budgets or negotiate some sort of solution amongst themselves in order to eliminate dispute.

Income Taxes

Each year the opposing parent gets to claim the child on their taxes from the year before. It is to be an even equal opportunity for each parent. Past years has been the first year-mother, second year-Grandfather, third year-Father, Fourth year- Father. Leaving the next year to be Mother; unless there is an agreement made between the two parties. The following years to come must also be given appropriately as to give fair chance to claim the child on their income taxes. However, a portion of the amount claimed
should be negotiated between the mediators and the parental guardians over the child.

THE LAST LIVING WILL TO ACT AS CARETAKER

Given right to Authority

LIFE IN A TRAGEDY SITUATION OF DEATH

AS LIFE SOMETIMES HAS UNFORTUNATE EVENTS TAKEN PLACE, FAMILIES EVERYDAY ARE LEFT WITH RESPONSIBILITIES EVEN AFTER PEOPLE DIE. ALTHOUGH THIS IS AN UNFORTUNATE EVENT THAT NO ONE HOPES WOULD TAKE PLACE, THIS AGREEMENT HAS PROCEDURES AND GUIDELINES TO FOLLOW AS THE LAST LIVING WILL FOR THE CHILD. IF ANYTHING SHOULD HAPPEN TO EITHER LEGAL CUSTODIAL GUARDIAN OF THE TWO PARTY THEIR RIGHTS SHOULD THEN BE PASSED ALONG TO THE NEXT OF KIN. WHICH INTRODUCES THE GRANDMOTHERS OF THE CHILD. CARLA WILLIAMSON IS GRANTED FULL AUTHORITY OVER THE CHILD IF GOD FORBID ANYTHING SUCH AS DEATH SHOULD HAPPEN. LEGAL RIGHT THEN WOULD BE SHARED WITH CARLA ALONG WITH THE LIVING MOTHER. VICE VERSA IF GOD FORBID ANYTHING SHOULD EVER HAPPEN SUCH AS DEATH WITH COURTNEY, THEN THEN RUSHELL WHOM OF WHICH IS THE GRANDMOTHER WOULD THEN SHARE HER RIGHTS WITH THE STILL LIVING FATHER.

SITUATIONS PERTAINING TO A TEMPORARY LEAVE OF PARENTAL ABSENCE.

THIS SHOULD TAKE EFFECT IF ONE OR BOTH LEGAL PARENTAL CUSTODIANS OVER THE MINOR CHILD HAS TO TAKE A LEAVE OF ABSENCE AND WAIVE THERE PARENTAL RIGHTS OVER THE CHILD AS A TEMPORARY LEAVE OF PARENTAL ABSENCE. A TEMPORARY LEAVE OF PARENTAL ABSENCE MAY BE DUE TO ILLNESS, ACCIDENTAL, ADVANCE OPPORTUNITY PURPOSES, EMPLOYMENT, EDUCATIONAL, INCARCERATION OR ETC. THE SAME PROCEDURES AND GUIDELINES PRESENTED ABOVE ARE TO BE TAKEN INTO EFFECT, BUT ONLY AS A TEMPORARY FULL POWER 2OF ATTORNEY. THE GRANDPARENTS OF THE CHILD HEREBY TAKE FULL RIGHTS AND RESPONSIBILITIES TO SHARE ALONG WITH THE CURRENT OPPOSING PARTY THAT IS CONSIDERED THE PRESENT GUARDIAN OVER THE MINOR CHILD. THIS TEMPORARY POWER OF ATTORNEY TAKES EFFECT UNTIL THE FULL TERM OF ABSENCE IS NO LONGER AN ISSUE. ONCE THE PARENTAL CUSTODIAL GUARDIAN IS AGAIN ABLE TO ACT AS CARE GIVER, THEN THEY ARE GIVEN BACK THERE PARENTAL RIGHTS AT ANY GIVEN TIME. THE GRANDPARENT THEN IS GRANTED THE TITLE AS A MEDIATOR AGAIN.

ESTABLISHING THE LAST LIVING WILL TO ACT AS CARE TAKER

BY GIVING YOUR SIGNATURE YOU ARE ACKNOWLEDGING IN FACT, TO UNDERSTANDING THE INFORMATION UNDER; "THE LAST LIVING WILL TO ACT AS CARE TAKER" SECTION OF THIS AGREEMENT. WITHOUT SIGNING THIS PART OF THE AGREEMENT AND SOMETHING UNFORTUNATE WERE TO

HAPPEN, THEN THE OTHER PARTY COULD RECEIVE FULL RIGHTS TO THE CHILD. THIS ISN'T IMPLYING THE WORST OF SITUATION OF HAVING CHANCE TO TAKING PLACE, SUCH AS THE OTHER PARTY TAKING FULL AUTHORITY OVER THE CHILD AND USING IT TO ITS FULL CAPABILITY TO

OVERRULING THE LEGAL RIGHT TO VISITATION AND/OR RESIDENTIAL ARRANGEMENT OF HAPPENING. HOWEVER, THIS IS TO DOCUMENT THE LAST LIVING WILL AS CARETAKER MADE BY THE TWO PARTIES DECISION

IF ANY TRAGEDY HAPPENS TO THE CUSTODIANS OF THIS CHILD. ALSO ESTABLISHING WHAT RIGHTS THEY HAVE OVER THE CHILD IF GOD FORBID ANYTHING SHOULD HAPPEN.

ONE OUT OF THE TWO PARTY

X_____ DATE _____

(MOTHERS SIGNATURE)

X_____ DATE _____

(PERSON GIVEN FULL AUTHORITY POWER OF ATTORNEY SHOULD ANYTHING HAPPEN)

THE OTHER ONE OUT OF THE TWO PARTY

X_____ DATE _____

(FATHERS SIGNATURE)

X_____ DATE _____

(PERSON GIVEN FULL AUTHORITY POWER OF ATTORNEY SHOULD ANYTHING HAPPEN)

Pᴀʀᴇɴᴛᴀʟ sᴜᴘᴘᴏʀᴛ

Terminology

Order to reaffirm our commitment of raising our child in a dual household status, we choose to use the terms "live with mother" and "live with father" in describing our arrangement, rather than in terms of custody/primary and non-custodial/access as may be defined in other legal documents. As parents, we both recognize that each of our contributions toward our child well-being is genuine. We further agree to cooperate with one another in to establish mutually acceptable standards for the development, education, health, and discipline of our child; to share in major decision-making events which may include but is not limited to medical, dental, and psychological treatment, grade and special program placement, change of schools, and legal issues; to acknowledge that day-to-day decisions for the child will be the responsibility of the parent in residence; and to respect any differences we have in our parenting techniques and reasonably attempt to reconcile those differences in the best interests of our child

Access & Communication

We expressly agree that except in the event of illness, injury, or other form of emergency, we will not deny our child access to the other parent during their scheduled period as a form of punishment or acceptance of the child's preference to cancel. Moreover, neither parent will schedule activities which conflict with the other parents time with the child, however, if one parent has plans for the child that are conflicting, we hereby consent to arrive at an agreeable resolution. We each agree to respect our child's right to privacy, and shall not spy on the child or other parent in the exchange of phone calls, e-mails, and postal letters, of otherwise interfere with personal communications. Packages, cards, gifts and other items shall be delivered unopened to the child as addressed, and for the purpose to which it was made, (i.e. Christmas, birthday, graduation) or other celebratory occasion as may be specified by the giving parent.   To all of which, we further expressly agree to review and renegotiate in good faith, any and all modifications to the shared parenting access schedules in concert with the changing ages of our child, and as other important circumstances may occur.

Discipline and Reward:

We agree that consistency in methods of discipline and reward are important to ensuring responsible parenting and the healthy development of our child. We further understand that child guidance requires flexibility and encouragement as equally well as enforced rules and restrictions to allow our child to receive the maximum benefit of love, concern, nurturing, and safety from both the mother and father.

In acceptance of this accord, we agree to discuss and support joint decisions relative to our child's growth and development, and will not subvert or supplant pronouncements of same. The administration of corporal punishment shall be severely restricted and used only as jointly agreed in matters of discipline and guidance. Neither will we offer unreasonable rewards to bribe good behavior, or create unfair or competitive circumstances of one parent over another.

Acknowledging Our Responsibility

In the event, our child should create a financial or legal liability, either through accident or acts of negligence, vandalism, or malicious mischief to persons or property, we agree to be equally responsible for the conduct of our child.

To REPRESENT A PARTY WITH A NOTION

THIS PAGE IS ONLY TO BE SIGNED IF THERE HAS BEEN A NOTION MADE TO CHANGE OR MODIFY THIS LEGAL BINDING AGREEMENT

IF YOU ARE STILL IN AGREEMENT TO THIS DOCUMENT IGNORE THIS PAGE. OTHERWISE PROCEED TO THE FOLLOWING:

PROPOSE A NOTION WITH REASON AND BACKING BY PLACING YOUR SIGNITURE TO REPRESENT THE VOICE OF THIS NOTION. PLEASE DESCRIBE THE ISSUE YOU WISH TO BE CHANGED PERMINANTLY. FORMALLY SEEKING THAT AN ISSUE BE NOTICED AND IF SECONDED BY THE OTHER PARTY, CONDUCT A FOLLOW THROUGH BY EDITTING THIS LEGAL DOCUMENT. TO CONFORM A NEWLY IMPROVED LEGAL BINDING AGREEMENT TO BE REPRESENTED AS A FOLLOWING VOLUME TO A SERIES.

IF YOU CANNOT COME TO AN AGREEMENT AND IT'S A TIE BETWEEN MEDIATORS THEN THE DISPUTE MAY HAVE TO BE FILED IN THE COURT OF LAW INFRONT OF A JUDGE TO END ALL DISPUTE. IF THIS HAPPENS THIS DOCUMENT MUST STILL BE USED AS A REFERENCE, AS IT'S ALREADY BEEN SIGNED AS a LEGAL BINDING AGREEMENT BETWEEN A TWO PARTIES DECISION.

YOU'RE NOTION

_____

_____   _____

_____

_____

---THE REASON BEHIND YOUR DECISION TO MAKING THIS NOTION ----

_____

_____

_____

_____

_____

Signature: _____ by the person making this

notion. Date of notion: _____

Signature: _____ Made by the opposing party stating that they have read the notion. Also representing acknowledgment to having a mutual agreement for the notion to be put into motion for the future establishment of A LEGAL BINDING AGREEMENT VOLUME II.

.
Date to motion: _____

Expected release date to volume II of The Legal Binding Agreement_____

RESOURCES---

Child Support Enforcement-The Division of Child Support Enforcement (DCSE) is a division within the Department of Social Services. DCSE works in partnership with the Federal Office of Child Support Enforcement and other State agencies. The actions of DCSE are based on federal and state law.The primary goal of DCSE is to work with parents and guardians to help establish.

Child Support is an obligation of a parent to provide emotional, financial, and medical support for a child or children. DCFS offers parent locator and paternity establishment services, as well as assistance to establish and enforce child support orders and collection and distribution of child support payments.

Anyone who receives FITAP, KCSP, or is referred to DCFS by Medicaid automatically receives child support enforcement services.

Child Support awards are established by combined monthly adjusted income.

$0 - $4,999 ; $5,000 - $12,999 ; $13,000 - $19,999 ; Above $20,000

Payments should be made by money order or cashier's check and mailed to:

Centralized Collection Unit

Post Office Box 260222

Baton Rouge, LA 70826

Payments should be made payable to the Department of Children and Family Services (DCFS) and Include the payor's name, address, and social security number and/or LASES number.

Also A Special Thanks To The Following, For The EASE OF ACCESS TO SELF PUBLISHING THIS, "LEGAL BINDIING AGREEMENT." ADOBE ACROBAT PRO DC- BY ALLOWING ME TO CONVERT TEXT TO PDF, AS WELL AS EDIT THE PDF FILE AS A TEXT FORMATED FILE. ELIMINATING AS MANY CONVERTING FILE FORMATS INBETWEEN, TO ESTABLISH THE ACTUAL TO MY OWN STANDARDS OF AN ACCEPTIABLE PROOF DIGITAL COPY AND FORMATED PDF FILE FOR PUBLISHING. CREATESPACE- AFTER MANY PRIOR READ COPIES, SOME OF WHICH PASSED THEIR ACCEPTANCE AND APPROVAL FOR PUBLISHING AND SOME THAT DIDN'T OVERALL GAIN MY OWN OPINON OF A SELF PUBLISHED FILE FORMAT OF A LEGAL BINDING AGREEMENT . OVERALL, ALLOWING MY OWN SELF PUBLICATION. MICROSOFT OFFICE-GIVING ME THE TOOLS TO CREATE A BLANK PAGE INTO THIS.

THINGS TO DO

→ _____
→ _____
→ _____
→ _____
→ _____
→ _____
→ _____
→ _____
→ _____
→ _____
→ _____
→ _____
→ _____
→ _____
→ _____
→ _____
→ _____
→ _____
→ _____
→ _____
→ _____
→ _____
→ _____
→ _____
→ _____
→ _____
→ _____
→ _____
→ _____

THINGS TO DO

→ _____
→ _____
→ _____
→ _____
→ _____
→ _____
→ _____
→ _____
→ _____
→ _____
→ _____
→ _____
→ _____
→ _____
→ _____
→ _____
→ _____
→ _____
→ _____
→ _____
→ _____
→ _____
→ _____
→ _____
→ _____
→ _____
→ _____
→ _____
→ _____
→ _____
→ _____

THINGS TO DO

→ _____
→ _____
→ _____
→ _____
→ _____
→ _____
→ _____
→ _____
→ _____
→ _____
→ _____
→ _____
→ _____
→ _____
→ _____
→ _____
→ _____
→ _____
→ _____
→ _____
→ _____
→ _____
→ _____
→ _____
→ _____
→ _____
→ _____
→ _____

CONTACT LIST

NAME/COMPANY	#	ADDRESS		
Note:				
NAME/COMPANY	#	ADDRESS		
Note:				
NAME/COMPANY	#	ADDRESS		
Note:				
NAME/COMPANY	#	ADDRESS		
Note:				
NAME/COMPANY	#	ADDRESS		
Note:				
NAME/COMPANY	#	ADDRESS		
Note:				
NAME/COMPANY	#	ADDRESS		
Note:				
NAME/COMPANY	#	ADDRESS		
Note:				
NAME/COMPANY	#	ADDRESS		
Note:				
NAME/COMPANY	#	ADDRESS		
Note				

CONTACT LIST

NAME/COMPANY	#	ADDRESS		
Note:				
NAME/COMPANY	#	ADDRESS		
Note:				
NAME/COMPANY	#	ADDRESS		
Note:				
NAME/COMPANY	#	ADDRESS		
Note:				
NAME/COMPANY	#	ADDRESS		
Note:				
NAME/COMPANY	#	ADDRESS		
Note:				
NAME/COMPANY	#	ADDRESS		
Note:				
NAME/COMPANY	#	ADDRESS		
Note:				
NAME/COMPANY	#	ADDRESS		
Note:				
NAME/COMPANY	#	ADDRESS		
Note				

Certificate Of Appreciation

Presented to

Every Person Listed In This Agreement

For volunteering time and effort
Put into a wonderful and simple man in the making
Thanks to volunteers like you, the children of our
City become better citizens worth knowing

A blessed mother's signature

February 2016

A more than happy father's signature

2016

JANUARY

S	M	T	W	T	F	S
					1	2
3	4	5	6	7	8	9
10	11	12	13	14	15	16
17	18	19	20	21	22	23
24	25	26	27	28	29	30
31						

JULY

S	M	T	W	T	F	S
					1	2
3	4	5	6	7	8	9
10	11	12	13	14	15	16
17	18	19	20	21	22	23
24	25	26	27	28	29	30
31						

FEBRUARY

1	2	3	4	5	6	
7	8	9	10	11	12	13
14	15	16	17	18	19	20
21	22	23	24	25	26	27
28	29					

AUGUST

1	2	3	4	5	6	
7	8	9	10	11	12	13
14	15	16	17	18	19	20
21	22	23	24	25	26	27
28	29	30	31			

MARCH

1	2	3	4	5		
6	7	8	9	10	11	12
13	14	15	16	17	18	19
20	21	22	23	24	25	26
27	28	29	30	31		

SEPTEMBER

1	2	3				
4	5	6	7	8	9	10
11	12	13	14	15	16	17
18	19	20	21	22	23	24
25	26	27	28	29	30	

APRIL

1	2					
3	4	5	6	7	8	9
10	11	12	13	14	15	16
17	18	19	20	21	22	23
24	25	26	27	28	29	30

OCTOBER

						1
2	3	4	5	6	7	8
9	10	11	12	13	14	15
16	17	18	19	20	21	22
23	24	25	26	27	28	29
30	31					

MAY

1	2	3	4	5	6	7
8	9	10	11	12	13	14
15	16	17	18	19	20	21
22	23	24	25	26	27	28
29	30	31				

NOVEMBER

		1	2	3	4	5
6	7	8	9	10	11	12
13	14	15	16	17	18	19
20	21	22	23	24	25	26
27	28	29	30			

JUNE

			1	2	3	4
5	6	7	8	9	10	11
12	13	14	15	16	17	18
19	20	21	22	23	24	25
26	27	28	29	30		

DECEMBER

				1	2	3
4	5	6	7	8	9	10
11	12	13	14	15	16	17
18	19	20	21	22	23	24
25	26	27	28	29	30	31

2017

JANUARY
S	T	W	T	S
	2	3	4	5	6	7
8		10	11	12	13	14
15		17	18	19	20	21
22	23	24	25	26	27	28
29	30	31

JULY
S		W	T	F	S
					1
2	3		5	6	7	8
9	10	11	12	13	14	15
16	17	18	19	20	21	22
23	24	25	26	27	28	29

FEBRUARY
			1	2	3	4
5	6		8	9	10	11
12	13		15	16	17	18
19	20	21	22	23	24	25
26	27	28

AUGUST
	1	2	3	4	5
6	7	8	9	10	11	12
13	14	15	16	17	18	19
20	21	22	23	2	25	26
27	28	29	30	31

MARCH
			1	2	3	4
5	6	7	8	9	10	11
12	13	14	15	16	17	18
19	20	21	22	23	24	25
26	27	28	29	30	31

SEPTEMBER
					1	2
3	4	5	6	7	8	9
10	11	12	13	14	15	16
17	18	19	20	21	22	23
24	25	26	27	28	29	30

APRIL
						1
2	3	4	5	6		8
9	10	11	12	13		15
16	17	18	19	20	21	22
23	24	25	26	27	28	29
30

OCTOBER
1	2	3	4	5	6	7
8	9	10	11	12	13	14
15	16	17	18	19	20	21
22	23	24	25	26	27	28
29	30	31

APPOINTMENTS

MAY
1	2	3	4	5	6
7	8	9	10	11	12	13
	15	16	17	18	19	20
21	22	23	24	25	26	27
28	29	30	31

NOVEMBER
			1	2	3	4
5	6	7	8	9	10	11
12	13	14	15	16	17	18
19	20	21	22	23	24	25
26	27	28	29	30

JUNE
			1	2	3
4	5	6	7	8	9	10
11	12	13	14	15	16	17
	19	20	21	22	23	24
25	26	27	28	29	30

DECEMBER
					1	2
3	4	5	6	7	8	9
10	11	12	13	14	15	16
17	18	19	20	21	22	23
24	25	26	27	28	29	30
31

DATES FROM THE PAST, SINCE BIRTH.

2010

January
SUN	MON	TUE	WED	THU	FRI	SAT
					1	2
3	4	5	6	7	8	9
10	11	12	13	14	15	16
17	18	19	20	21	22	23
24/31	25	26	27	28	29	30

February
SUN	MON	TUE	WED	THU	FRI	SAT
	1	2	3	4	5	6
7	8	9	10	11	12	13
14	15	16	17	18	19	20
21	22	23	24	25	26	27
28						

March
SUN	MON	TUE	WED	THU	FRI	SAT
	1	2	3	4	5	6
7	8	9	10	11	12	13
14	15	16	17	18	19	20
21	22	23	24	25	26	27
28	29	30	31			

April
SUN	MON	TUE	WED	THU	FRI	SAT
				1	2	3
4	5	6	7	8	9	10
11	12	13	14	15	16	17
18	19	20	21	22	23	24
25	26	27	28	29	30	

May
SUN	MON	TUE	WED	THU	FRI	SAT
						1
2	3	4	5	6	7	8
9	10	11	12	13	14	15
16	17	18	19	20	21	22
23/30	24/31	25	26	27	28	29

June
SUN	MON	TUE	WED	THU	FRI	SAT
		1	2	3	4	5
6	7	8	9	10	11	12
13	14	15	16	17	18	19
20	21	22	23	24	25	26
27	28	29	30			

July
SUN	MON	TUE	WED	THU	FRI	SAT
				1	2	3
4	5	6	7	8	9	10
11	12	13	14	15	16	17
18	19	20	21	22	23	24
25	26	27	28	29	30	31

August
SUN	MON	TUE	WED	THU	FRI	SAT
1	2	3	4	5	6	7
8	9	10	11	12	13	14
15	16	17	18	19	20	21
22	23	24	25	26	27	28
29	30	31				

September
SUN	MON	TUE	WED	THU	FRI	SAT
			1	2	3	4
5	6	7	8	9	10	11
12	13	14	15	16	17	18
19	20	21	22	23	24	25
26	27	28	29	30		

October
SUN	MON	TUE	WED	THU	FRI	SAT
					1	2
3	4	5	6	7	8	9
10	11	12	13	14	15	16
17	18	19	20	21	22	23
24/31	25	26	27	28	29	30

November
SUN	MON	TUE	WED	THU	FRI	SAT
	1	2	3	4	5	6
7	8	9	10	11	12	13
14	15	16	17	18	19	20
21	22	23	24	25	26	27
28	29	30				

December
SUN	MON	TUE	WED	THU	FRI	SAT
			1	2	3	4
5	6	7	8	9	10	11
12	13	14	15	16	17	18
19	20	21	22	23	24	25
26	27	28	29	30	31	

Calendar 2011

JANUARY 2011
SUN	MON	TUES	WED	THURS	FRI	SAT
30	31					1
2	3	4	5	6	7	8
9	10	11	12	13	14	15
16	17	18	19	20	21	22
23	24	25	26	27	28	29

FEBRUARY 2011
SUN	MON	TUES	WED	THURS	FRI	SAT
	1	2	3	4	5	
6	7	8	9	10	11	12
13	14	15	16	17	18	19
20	21	22	23	24	25	26
27	28					

MARCH 2011
SUN	MON	TUES	WED	THURS	FRI	SAT
		1	2	3	4	5
6	7	8	9	10	11	12
13	14	15	16	17	18	19
20	21	22	23	24	25	26
27	28	29	30	31		

APRIL 2011
SUN	MON	TUES	WED	THURS	FRI	SAT
					1	2
3	4	5	6	7	8	9
10	11	12	13	14	15	16
17	18	19	20	21	22	23
24	25	26	27	28	29	30

MAY 2011
SUN	MON	TUES	WED	THURS	FRI	SAT
1	2	3	4	5	6	7
8	9	10	11	12	13	14
15	16	17	18	19	20	21
22	23	24	25	26	27	28
29	30	31				

JUNE 2011
SUN	MON	TUES	WED	THURS	FRI	SAT
			1	2	3	4
5	6	7	8	9	10	11
12	13	14	15	16	17	18
19	20	21	22	23	24	25
26	27	28	29	30		

JULY 2011
SUN	MON	TUES	WED	THURS	FRI	SAT
31					1	2
3	4	5	6	7	8	9
10	11	12	13	14	15	16
17	18	19	20	21	22	23
24	25	26	27	28	29	30

AUGUST 2011
SUN	MON	TUES	WED	THURS	FRI	SAT
	1	2	3	4	5	6
7	8	9	10	11	12	13
14	15	16	17	18	19	20
21	22	23	24	25	26	27
28	29	30	31			

SEPTEMBER 2011
SUN	MON	TUES	WED	THURS	FRI	SAT
				1	2	3
4	5	6	7	8	9	10
11	12	13	14	15	16	17
18	19	20	21	22	23	24
25	26	27	28	29	30	

OCTOBER 2011
SUN	MON	TUES	WED	THURS	FRI	SAT
30	31					1
2	3	4	5	6	7	8
9	10	11	12	13	14	15
16	17	18	19	20	21	22
23	24	25	26	27	28	29

NOVEMBER 2011
SUN	MON	TUES	WED	THURS	FRI	SAT
		1	2	3	4	5
6	7	8	9	10	11	12
13	14	15	16	17	18	19
20	21	22	23	24	25	26
27	28	29	30			

DECEMBER 2011
SUN	MON	TUES	WED	THURS	FRI	SAT
				1	2	3
4	5	6	7	8	9	10
11	12	13	14	15	16	17
18	19	20	21	22	23	24
25	26	27	28	29	30	31

2012

JANUARY
Su	Mo	Tu	We	Th	Fr	Sa
1	2	3	4	5	6	7
8	9	10	11	12	13	14
15	16	17	18	19	20	21
22	23	24	25	26	27	28
29	30	31				

FEBRUARY
Su	Mo	Tu	We	Th	Fr	Sa
			1	2	3	4
5	6	7	8	9	10	11
12	13	14	15	16	17	18
19	20	21	22	23	24	25
26	27	28	29			

MARCH
Su	Mo	Tu	We	Th	Fr	Sa
				1	2	3
4	5	6	7	8	9	10
11	12	13	14	15	16	17
18	19	20	21	22	23	24
25	26	27	28	29	30	31

APRIL
Su	Mo	Tu	We	Th	Fr	Sa
1	2	3	4	5	6	7
8	9	10	11	12	13	14
15	16	17	18	19	20	21
22	23	24	25	26	27	28
29	30					

MAY
Su	Mo	Tu	We	Th	Fr	Sa
		1	2	3	4	5
6	7	8	9	10	11	12
13	14	15	16	17	18	19
20	21	22	23	24	25	26
27	28	29	30	31		

JUNE
Su	Mo	Tu	We	Th	Fr	Sa
					1	2
3	4	5	6	7	8	9
10	11	12	13	14	15	16
17	18	19	20	21	22	23
24	25	26	27	28	29	30

JULY
Su	Mo	Tu	We	Th	Fr	Sa
1	2	3	4	5	6	7
8	9	10	11	12	13	14
15	16	17	18	19	20	21
22	23	24	25	26	27	28
29	30	31				

AUGUST
Su	Mo	Tu	We	Th	Fr	Sa
			1	2	3	4
5	6	7	8	9	10	11
12	13	14	15	16	17	18
19	20	21	22	23	24	25
26	27	28	29	30	31	

SEPTEMBER
Su	Mo	Tu	We	Th	Fr	Sa
						1
2	3	4	5	6	7	8
9	10	11	12	13	14	15
16	17	18	19	20	21	22
23	24	25	26	27	28	29
30						

OCTOBER
Su	Mo	Tu	We	Th	Fr	Sa
	1	2	3	4	5	6
7	8	9	10	11	12	13
14	15	16	17	18	19	20
21	22	23	24	25	26	27
28	29	30	31			

NOVEMBER
Su	Mo	Tu	We	Th	Fr	Sa
				1	2	3
4	5	6	7	8	9	10
11	12	13	14	15	16	17
18	19	20	21	22	23	24
25	26	27	28	29	30	

DECEMBER
Su	Mo	Tu	We	Th	Fr	Sa
						1
2	3	4	5	6	7	8
9	10	11	12	13	14	15
16	17	18	19	20	21	22
23	24	25	26	27	28	29
30	31					

www.callmevictorian.com

2013

January
S	M	T	W	T	F	S
		1	2	3	4	5
6	7	8	9	10	11	12
13	14	15	16	17	18	19
20	21	22	23	24	25	26
27	28	29	30	31		

February
S	M	T	W	T	F	S
					1	2
3	4	5	6	7	8	9
10	11	12	13	14	15	16
17	18	19	20	21	22	23
24	25	26	27	28		

March
S	M	T	W	T	F	S
					1	2
3	4	5	6	7	8	9
10	11	12	13	14	15	16
17	18	19	20	21	22	23
24	25	26	27	28	29	30
31						

April
S	M	T	W	T	F	S
	1	2	3	4	5	6
7	8	9	10	11	12	13
14	15	16	17	18	19	20
21	22	23	24	25	26	27
28	29	30				

May
S	M	T	W	T	F	S
			1	2	3	4
5	6	7	8	9	10	11
12	13	14	15	16	17	18
19	20	21	22	23	24	25
26	27	28	29	30	31	

June
S	M	T	W	T	F	S
						1
2	3	4	5	6	7	8
9	10	11	12	13	14	15
16	17	18	19	20	21	22
23	24	25	26	27	28	29
30						

July
S	M	T	W	T	F	S
	1	2	3	4	5	6
7	8	9	10	11	12	13
14	15	16	17	18	19	20
21	22	23	24	25	26	27
28	29	30	31			

August
S	M	T	W	T	F	S
				1	2	3
4	5	6	7	8	9	10
11	12	13	14	15	16	17
18	19	20	21	22	23	24
25	26	27	28	29	30	31

September
S	M	T	W	T	F	S
1	2	3	4	5	6	7
8	9	10	11	12	13	14
15	16	17	18	19	20	21
22	23	24	25	26	27	28
29	30					

October
S	M	T	W	T	F	S
		1	2	3	4	5
6	7	8	9	10	11	12
13	14	15	16	17	18	19
20	21	22	23	24	25	26
27	28	29	30	31		

November
S	M	T	W	T	F	S
					1	2
3	4	5	6	7	8	9
10	11	12	13	14	15	16
17	18	19	20	21	22	23
24	25	26	27	28	29	30

December
S	M	T	W	T	F	S
1	2	3	4	5	6	7
8	9	10	11	12	13	14
15	16	17	18	19	20	21
22	23	24	25	26	27	28
29	30	31				

2014

JANUARY
S	M	T	W	T	F	S
			1	2	3	4
5	6	7	8	9	10	11
12	13	14	15	16	17	18
19	20	21	22	23	24	25
26	27	28	29	30	31	

FEBRUARY
S	M	T	W	T	F	S
						1
2	3	4	5	6	7	8
9	10	11	12	13	14	15
16	17	18	19	20	21	22
23	24	25	26	27	28	

MARCH
S	M	T	W	T	F	S
						1
2	3	4	5	6	7	8
9	10	11	12	13	14	15
16	17	18	19	20	21	22
23	24	25	26	27	28	29
30	31					

APRIL
S	M	T	W	T	F	S
		1	2	3	4	5
6	7	8	9	10	11	12
13	14	15	16	17	18	19
20	21	22	23	24	25	26
27	28	29	30			

MAY
S	M	T	W	T	F	S
				1	2	3
4	5	6	7	8	9	10
11	12	13	14	15	16	17
18	19	20	21	22	23	24
25	26	27	28	29	30	31

JUNE
S	M	T	W	T	F	S
1	2	3	4	5	6	7
8	9	10	11	12	13	14
15	16	17	18	19	20	21
22	23	24	25	26	27	28
29	30					

JULY
S	M	T	W	T	F	S
		1	2	3	4	5
6	7	8	9	10	11	12
13	14	15	16	17	18	19
20	21	22	23	24	25	26
27	28	29	30	31		

AUGUST
S	M	T	W	T	F	S
					1	2
3	4	5	6	7	8	9
10	11	12	13	14	15	16
17	18	19	20	21	22	23
24	25	26	27	28	29	30
31						

SEPTEMBER
S	M	T	W	T	F	S
	1	2	3	4	5	6
7	8	9	10	11	12	13
14	15	16	17	18	19	20
21	22	23	24	25	26	27
28	29	30				

OCTOBER
S	M	T	W	T	F	S
			1	2	3	4
5	6	7	8	9	10	11
12	13	14	15	16	17	18
19	20	21	22	23	24	25
26	27	28	29	30	31	

NOVEMBER
S	M	T	W	T	F	S
						1
2	3	4	5	6	7	8
9	10	11	12	13	14	15
16	17	18	19	20	21	22
23	24	25	26	27	28	29
30						

DECEMBER
S	M	T	W	T	F	S
	1	2	3	4	5	6
7	8	9	10	11	12	13
14	15	16	17	18	19	20
21	22	23	24	25	26	27
28	29	30	31			

2 0 1 5

January
Su	Mo	Tu	We	Th	Fr	Sa
				1	2	3
4	5	6	7	8	9	10
11	12	13	14	15	16	17
18	19	20	21	22	23	24
25	26	27	28	29	30	31

February
Su	Mo	Tu	We	Th	Fr	Sa
1	2	3	4	5	6	7
8	9	10	11	12	13	14
15	16	17	18	19	20	21
22	23	24	25	26	27	28

March
Su	Mo	Tu	We	Th	Fr	Sa
1	2	3	4	5	6	7
8	9	10	11	12	13	14
15	16	17	18	19	20	21
22	23	24	25	26	27	28
29	30	31				

April
Su	Mo	Tu	We	Th	Fr	Sa
			1	2	3	4
5	6	7	8	9	10	11
12	13	14	15	16	17	18
19	20	21	22	23	24	25
26	27	28	29	30		

May
Su	Mo	Tu	We	Th	Fr	Sa
31					1	2
3	4	5	6	7	8	9
10	11	12	13	14	15	16
17	18	19	20	21	22	23
24	25	26	27	28	29	30

June
Su	Mo	Tu	We	Th	Fr	Sa
	1	2	3	4	5	6
7	8	9	10	11	12	13
14	15	16	17	18	19	20
21	22	23	24	25	26	27
28	29	30				

July
Su	Mo	Tu	We	Th	Fr	Sa
			1	2	3	4
5	6	7	8	9	10	11
12	13	14	15	16	17	18
19	20	21	22	23	24	25
26	27	28	29	30	31	

August
Su	Mo	Tu	We	Th	Fr	Sa
30	31					1
2	3	4	5	6	7	8
9	10	11	12	13	14	15
16	17	18	19	20	21	22
23	24	25	26	27	28	29

September
Su	Mo	Tu	We	Th	Fr	Sa
		1	2	3	4	5
6	7	8	9	10	11	12
13	14	15	16	17	18	19
20	21	22	23	24	25	26
27	28	29	30			

October
Su	Mo	Tu	We	Th	Fr	Sa
				1	2	3
4	5	6	7	8	9	10
11	12	13	14	15	16	17
18	19	20	21	22	23	24
25	26	27	28	29	30	31

November
Su	Mo	Tu	We	Th	Fr	Sa
1	2	3	4	5	6	7
8	9	10	11	12	13	14
15	16	17	18	19	20	21
22	23	24	25	26	27	28
29	30					

December
Su	Mo	Tu	We	Th	Fr	Sa
		1	2	3	4	5
6	7	8	9	10	11	12
13	14	15	16	17	18	19
20	21	22	23	24	25	26
27	28	29	30	31		

Notes

Notes

Notes

CONTACT THE
AUTHOR
WITH THESE
QR CODES

The Selfish Giant
by Oscar Wilde
Every afternoon, as they were coming from school, the children used to
go and play in the Giant's garden.

It was a large lovely garden, with soft green grass. Here and there over
the grass stood beautiful flowers like stars, and there were twelve peach-
trees that in the spring-time broke out into delicate blossoms of pink and
pearl, and in the autumn bore rich fruit. The birds sat on the trees and
sang so sweetly that the children used to stop their games in order to listen
to them. "How happy we are here!" they cried to each other.

One day the Giant came back. He had been to visit his friend the Cornish
ogre, and had stayed with him for seven years. After the seven years were
over he had said all that he had to say, for his conversation was limited,
and he determined to return to his own castle. When he arrived he saw the
children playing in the garden.

"What are you doing here?" he cried in a very gruff voice, and the
children ran away.

"My own garden is my own garden," said the Giant; "any one can
understand that, and I will allow nobody to play in it but myself." So he
built a high wall all round it, and put up a notice-board.

TRESPASSERS
WILL BE
PROSECUTED

.

He was a very selfish Giant.

The poor children had now nowhere to play. They tried to play on the road, but the road was very dusty and full of hard stones, and they did not like it. They used to wander round the high wall when their lessons were over, and talk about the beautiful garden inside. "How happy we were there," they said to each other.

Then the Spring came, and all over the country there were little blossoms and little birds. Only in the garden of the Selfish Giant it was still winter. The birds did not care to sing in it as there were no children, and the trees forgot to blossom. Once a beautiful flower put its head out from the grass, but when it saw the notice-board it was so sorry for the children that it slipped back into the ground again, and went off to sleep. The only people who were pleased were the Snow and the Frost. "Spring has forgotten this garden," they cried, "so we will live here all the year round." The Snow covered up the grass with her great white cloak, and the Frost painted all the trees silver. Then they invited the North Wind to stay with them, and he came. He was wrapped in furs, and he roared all day about the garden, and blew the chimney-pots down. "This is a delightful spot," he said, "we must ask the Hail on a visit." So the Hail came. Every day for three hours he rattled on the roof of the castle till he broke most of the slates, and then he ran round and round the garden as fast as he could go. He was dressed in grey, and his breath was like ice

"I cannot understand why the Spring is so late in coming," said the Selfish Giant, as he sat at the window and looked out at his cold white garden; "I hope there will be a change in the weather."

But the Spring never came, nor the Summer. The Autumn gave golden fruit to every garden, but to the Giant's garden she gave none. "He is too selfish," she said. So it was always Winter there, and the North Wind, and the Hail, and the Frost, and the Snow danced about through the trees.

One morning the Giant was lying awake in bed when he heard some lovely music. It sounded so sweet to his ears that he thought it must be the King's musicians passing by. It was really only a little linnet singing outside his window, but it was so long since he had heard a bird sing in his garden that it seemed to him to be the most beautiful music in the world. Then the Hail stopped dancing over his head, and the North Wind ceased roaring, and a delicious perfume came to him through the open casement. "I believe the Spring has come at last," said the Giant; and he jumped out of bed and looked out.
What did he see?

He saw a most wonderful sight. Through a little hole in the wall the children had crept in, and they were sitting in the branches of the trees. In every tree that he could see there was a little child. And the trees were so glad to have the children back again that they had covered themselves with blossoms, and were waving their arms gently above the children's heads. The birds were flying about and twittering with delight, and the flowers were looking up through the green grass and laughing. It was a lovely scene, only in one corner it was still winter. It was the farthest corner of the garden, and in it was standing a little boy. He was so small that he could not reach up to the branches of the tree, and he was wandering all round it, crying bitterly. The poor tree was still quite covered with frost and snow, and the North Wind was blowing and roaring above it. "Climb up! little boy," said the Tree, and it bent its branches down as low as it could; but the boy was too tiny.

And the Giant's heart melted as he looked out. "How
selfish I have been!" he said; "now I know why the Spring would not
come here. I will put that poor little boy on the top of the tree, and then I
will knock down the wall, and
my garden shall be the children's playground for ever and ever." He was
really very sorry for what he had done.

So he crept downstairs and opened the front door quite softly, and went
out into the garden. But when the children saw him they were so
frightened that they all ran away, and the garden became winter again.
Only the little boy did not run, for his eyes were so full of tears that he
did not see the Giant coming. And the Giant stole up behind him and
took him gently in his hand, and put him up into the tree. And the tree
broke at once into blossom, and the birds came and sang on it, and the
little boy stretched out his two arms and flung them round the Giant's
neck, and kissed him. And the other children, when they saw that the
Giant was not wicked any longer, came running back, and with them
came the Spring. "It is your garden now, little children," said the Giant,
and he took a great axe and knocked down the wall. And when the
people were going to market at twelve o'clock they found the Giant
playing with the children in the most beautiful garden they had ever seen.

All day long they played, and in the evening they came to the Giant to
bid him good-bye.

"But where is your little companion?" he said: "the boy I put into the
tree." The Giant loved him the best because he had kissed him.

"We don't know," answered the children; "he has gone away."

"You must tell him to be sure and come here to-morrow," said the Giant.
But the children said that they did not know where he lived, and had
never seen him before; and the Giant felt very sad.

Every afternoon, when school was over, the children came and played with the Giant. But the little boy whom the Giant loved was never seen again. The Giant was very kind to all the children, yet he longed for his first little friend, and often spoke of him. "How I would like to see him!" he used to say.

Years went over, and the Giant grew very old and feeble. He could not play about any more, so he sat in a huge armchair, and watched the children at their games, and admired his garden. "I have many beautiful flowers," he said; "but the children are the most beautiful flowers of all."

One winter morning he looked out of his window as he was dressing. He did not hate the Winter now, for he knew that it was merely the Spring asleep, and that the flowers were resting.

Suddenly he rubbed his eyes in wonder, and looked and looked. It certainly was a marvellous sight. In the farthest corner of the garden was a tree quite covered with lovely white blossoms. Its branches were all golden, and silver fruit hung down from them, and underneath it stood the little boy he had loved.

Downstairs ran the Giant in great joy, and out into the garden. He hastened across the grass, and came near to the child. And when he came quite close his face grew red with anger, and he said, "Who hath dared to wound thee?" For on the palms of the child's hands were the prints of two nails, and the prints of two nails were on the little feet.

"Who hath dared to wound thee?" cried the Giant; "tell me, that I may take my big sword and slay him."

"Nay!" answered the child; "but these are the wounds of Love."

"Who art thou?" said the Giant, and a strange awe fell on him, and he knelt before the little child.

And the child smiled on the Giant, and said to him, "You let me play once in your garden, to-day you shall come with me to my garden, which is Paradise."

And when the children ran in that afternoon, they found the Giant lying dead under the tree, all covered with white blossoms.

THE END

Birth Day	Symbol	Modern Birth Stone	Traditional Stone	Mythical Stone	Planetary Stone
Capricorn (Dec. 22 - Jan. 19)	♑	Garnet	Garnet	Emerald	Lapis Lazuli
Aquarius (Jan. 20 - Feb. 18)	♒	Amethyst	Amethyst	Bloodstone	Turquoise
Pisces (Feb. 19 - Mar. 20)	♓	Aquamarine	Bloodstone	Jade	Aquamarine
Aries (Mar. 21 - Apr. 19)	♈	Diamond	Diamond	Opal	Jasper
Taurus (Apr. 20 - May 20)	♉	Emerald	Emerald	Sapphire	Emerald, Adventurine
Gemini (May 21 - Jun. 20)	♊	Pearl Moonstone	Alexandrite	Moonstone	Tiger Eye
Cancer (Jun. 21 - Jul. 22)	♋	Ruby	Ruby	Ruby	Moonstone
Leo (Jul. 23 - Aug. 22)	♌	Peridot	Sardonyx	Diamond	Rock Crystal
Virgo (Aug. 23 - Sep. 22)	♍	Sapphire	Sapphire	Agate	Citrine
Libra (Sep. 23 - Oct. 22)	♎	Opal Tourmaline	Tourmaline	Jasper	Sapphire
Scorpio (Oct. 23 - Nov. 21)	♏	Yellow Topaz Citrine	Citrine	Pearl	Garnet Ruby
Sagittarius (Nov. 22 - Dec. 21)	♐	Blue Topaz	Zircon, Turquoise, Lapis Lazuli	Black Onyx	Topaz

Weight			
grams	oz	grams	oz
10g	¼ oz	375g	13 oz
15g	½ oz	400g	14 oz
25g	1 oz	425g	15 oz
50g	1 ¾ oz	450g	1 lb
75g	2 ¾ oz	500g	1 lb 2 oz
100g	3 ½ oz	700g	1 ½ lb
150g	5 ½ oz	750g	1 lb 10 oz
175g	6 oz	1kg	2 ¼ lb
200g	7 oz	1.25kg	2 lb 12 oz
225g	8 oz	1.5kg	3 lb 5 oz
250g	9 oz	2kg	4 ½ lb
275g	9 ¾ oz	2.25kg	5 lb
300g	10 ½ oz	2.5kg	5 ½ lb
350g	12 oz	3kg	6 ½ lb

THE TEN COMMAND MENTS

GOD SPOKE THESE WORDS

1 YOU SHALL HAVE NO OTHER GODS BEFORE ME

2 YOU SHALL NOT MAKE FOR YOURSELF ANY GRAVEN IMAGE

3 YOU SHALL NOT TAKE THE NAME OF THE LORD IN VAIN

4 REMEMBER THE SABBATH DAY TO KEEP IT HOLY

5 HONOR YOUR FATHER AND MOTHER

6 YOU SHALL NOT MURDER

7 YOU SHALL NOT COMMIT ADULTERY

8 YOU SHALL NOT STEAL

9 YOU SHALL NOT BEAR FALSE WITNESS

10 YOU SHALL NOT COVET

Medical Arts Clinic

BJC Medical Group
of Missouri

1103 West Liberty Street , Farmington, MO 63640-1921
Tel: (573)756-6751 Fax: (573)756-6807

PATIENT:	Carson Tinsley	PCP:	Jeanne Kornhardt, MD
DOB:	08/18/2010	TODAY'S PROVIDER:	Jeanne M. Kornhardt MD
VISIT TYPE:	Office Visit	DATE:	10/21/2015 02:59 PM

Vaccine Administration Record

All Immunizations

Immunization	Completed Date
DTaP-IPV	9/3/2015 3:06:05 PM
MMR	9/3/2015 3:06:41 PM
Varicella	9/3/2015 3:07:00 PM
Hep A (ped/adol, 2 dose)	10/30/2012 1:14:00 PM
flu (split) preservative free, 6-35 mos	10/30/2012 1:15:00 PM
polio, inactivated (IPV)	2/25/2011 12:00:00 AM
polio, inactivated (IPV)	12/22/2010 12:00:00 AM
polio, inactivated (IPV)	10/22/2010 12:00:00 AM
HIB - unspecified	2/25/2011 12:00:00 AM
HIB - unspecified	12/22/2010 12:00:00 AM
HIB - unspecified	10/22/2010 12:00:00 AM
DTaP	2/25/2011 12:00:00 AM
DTaP	12/22/2010 12:00:00 AM
DTaP	10/22/2010 12:00:00 AM
hep B (ped/adol, 3 dose)	2/25/2011 12:00:00 AM
hep B (ped/adol, 3 dose)	12/22/2010 12:00:00 AM
hep B (ped/adol, 3 dose)	10/22/2010 12:00:00 AM
RotaTeq (Rotavirus 3 dose)	2/25/2011 12:00:00 AM
RotaTeq (Rotavirus 3 dose)	12/22/2010 12:00:00 AM
RotaTeq (Rotavirus 3 dose)	10/22/2010 12:00:00 AM
pneumo (under 5) (PCV13)	2/25/2011 12:00:00 AM
pneumo (under 5) (PCV7)	12/22/2010 12:00:00 AM
pneumo (under 5) (PCV7)	10/22/2010 12:00:00 AM
Pentacel	2/29/2012 10:50:00 AM
Hep A (ped/adol, 2 dose)	2/29/2012 10:51:00 AM
flu (split) preservative free, 6-35 mos	10/14/2011 2:55:00 PM
Varicella	10/14/2011 2:54:00 PM
MMR	10/14/2011 2:54:00 PM
PNEUMOCOCCAL 13-VALENT CONJUGATE VACCINE (DIPTHERIA CRM197 P	10/14/2011 2:54:00 PM

Jeanne M. Kornhardt MD
Jeanne M. Kornhardt MD

Document generated by : Natasha A. Pritchett 10/21/2015 03:47 PM

This Is How I Feel Today,

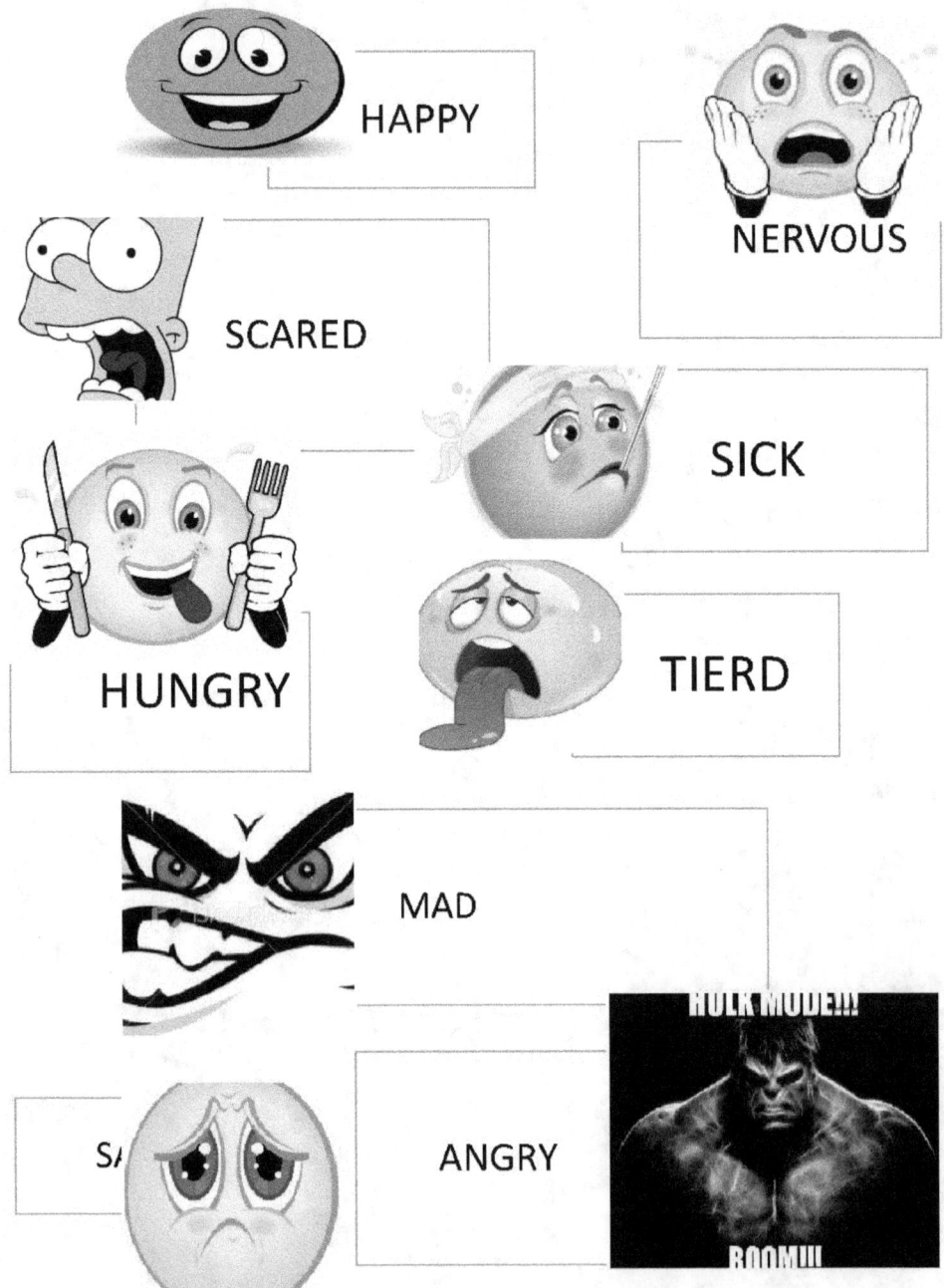

HAPPY

NERVOUS

SCARED

SICK

HUNGRY

TIERD

MAD

SA

ANGRY

Credit Memo

Date	Until	Name	Amount	Total

-------------------------- Meeting Minutes-------

Date:_____Time:_____
Discussion:_____
_____
_____
_____
_____
_____
_____

Goals:_____
_____
_____
_____

Next Intended Meeting:_____

------------------------------- Meeting Minutes--

Date:_____Time:_____
Discussion:_____
_____
_____
_____
_____
_____
_____

Goals:_____
_____
_____
_____

Next Intended Meeting:_____

------------------------- **Meeting Minutes**-------

Date:_____Time:_____
Discussion:_____
_____
_____
_____
_____
_____
_____

Goals:_____
_____
_____
_____

Next Intended Meeting:_____

------------------------------- **Meeting Minutes**--

Date:_____Time:_____
Discussion:_____
_____
_____
_____
_____
_____
_____

Goals:_____
_____
_____
_____

Next Intended Meeting:_____

----- Meeting Minutes-------------------------------

Date:_____Time:_____

Discussion:_____

_____

_____

_____

_____

_____

_____

Goals:_____

_____

_____

_____

Next Intended Meeting:_____

---------------- Meeting Minutes------------------

Date:_____Time:_____

Discussion:_____

_____

_____

_____

_____

_____

_____

Goals:_____

_____

_____

_____

Next Intended Meeting:_____

-------------------- Meeting Minutes-------------

Date:_____Time:_____
Discussion:_____
_____
_____
_____
_____
_____
_____

Goals:_____
_____
_____
_____

Next Intended Meeting:_____

------------------------------ Meeting Minutes-

Date:_____Time:_____
Discussion:_____
_____
_____
_____
_____
_____
_____

Goals:_____
_____
_____
_____

Next Intended Meeting:_____

American Sign Language Alphabet

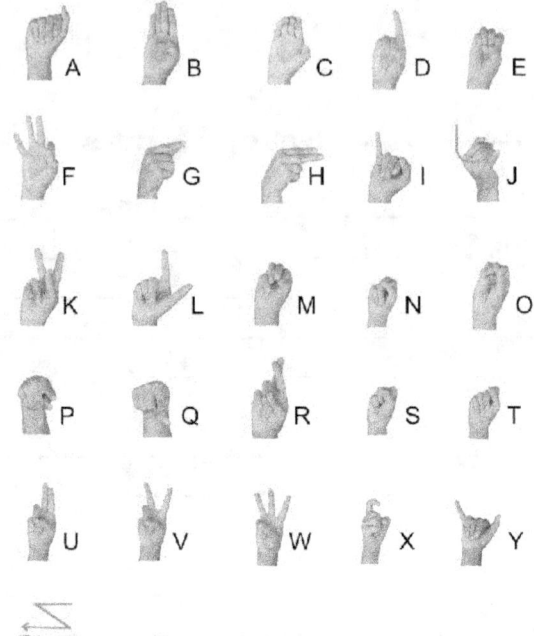

mom

dad

grandma

grandpa

sister

brother

aunt

uncle

52 WEEK MONEY SAVING CHALLENGE

MONEYSAVINGMADNESS.COM

Week	Amount Deposited	Balance	Done	Week	Amount Deposited	Balance	Done
1				27			
2				28			
3				29			
4				30			
5				31			
6				32			
7				33			
8				34			
9				35			
10				36			
11				37			
12				38			
13				39			
14				40			
15				41			
16				42			
17				43			
18				44			
19				45			
20				46			
21				47			
22				48			
23				49			
24				50			
25				51			
26				52			

my family tree

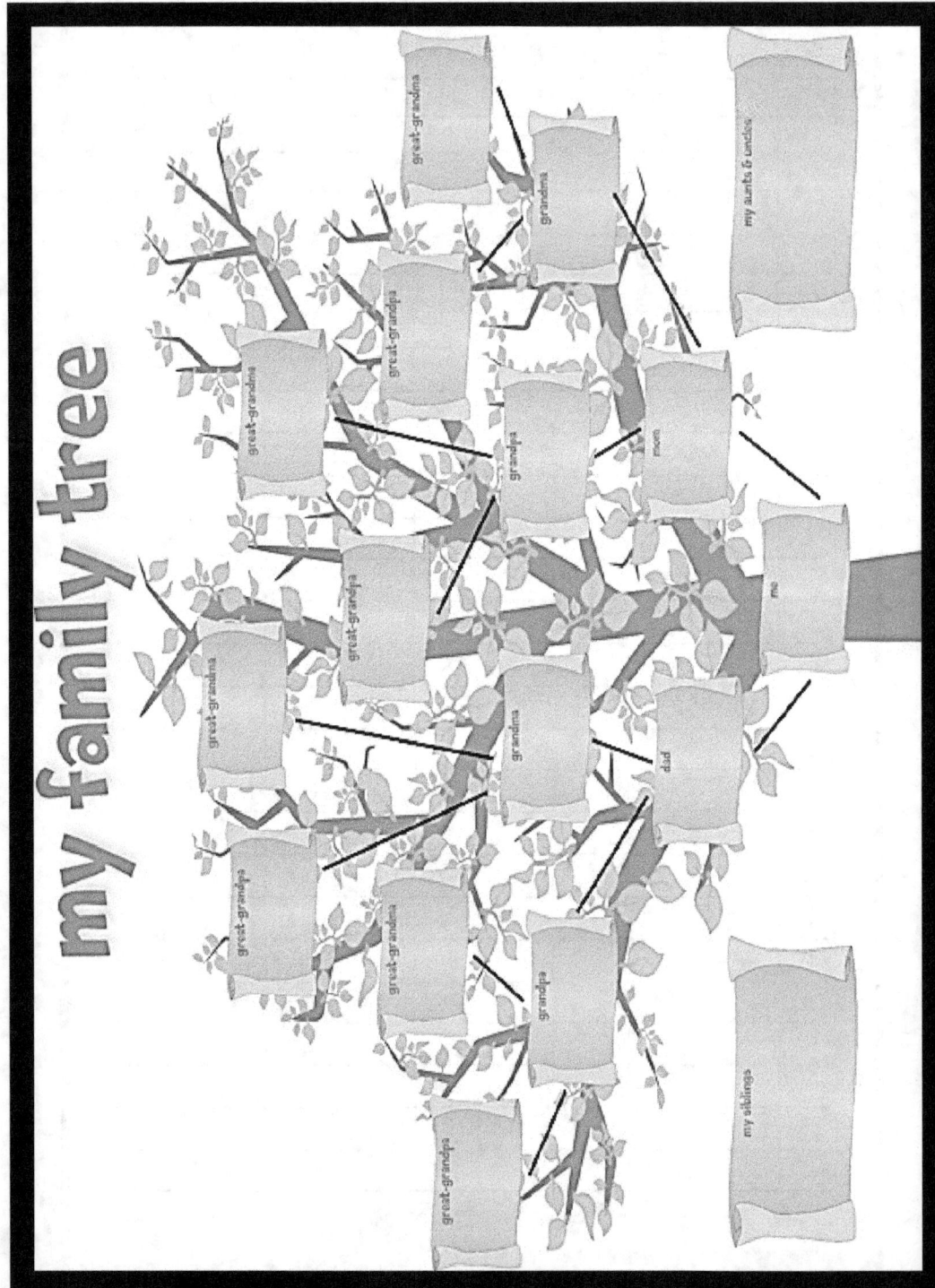

great-grandma

great-grandpa

great-grandma

great-grandpa

great-grandma

great-grandpa

great-grandma

great-grandpa

grandma

grandpa

grandma

grandpa

mom

dad

me

my aunts & uncles

my siblings

date	Payment method	Payment to	Description	Amount	subtotal	Note

date	Payment method	Payment to	Description	Amount	subtotal	Note

 Kids sticker chart

Kindergarten	First A	I Can Read	First Friend	First Sport	No more car seat!
First Girlfriend	First time I dressed myself	First time I tied my shoes	I cleaned my room, just me	Made you this!	A good influence!
cooked	Decide to go to church	Took the bus	Stayed all night with a friend	Taught you something you never knew	Built something
★	★		★★	★	★
★	★	★	★	★	★
	★★	★	★	★	★

www.ingramcontent.com/pod-product-compliance
Lightning Source LLC
Chambersburg PA
CBHW071231280526
45787CB00002B/878

* 9 7 8 1 5 1 8 8 7 6 5 7 8 *